# THE FIVE (5) FOLD MINISTRY

What is the church?

By

Ian McCormack

Published by

**KRATOS PUBLISHERS**

# THE FIVE FOLD MINISTRY

All bible scripture quotation are from authorized King James Version and unless otherwise indicated are taken from the English Standard Version.

Published By

**KRATOS PUBLISHERS**

# CONTENTS PAGE

INTRODUCTION ..................................................................4

BRIDE OF CHRIST..............................................................12

BODY OF CHRIST...............................................................15

THE BUILDING....................................................................21

YEARS IN MINISTRY..........................................................33

THE HAND...........................................................................40

THE PUZZLE.......................................................................44

OLD TESTAMENT STRUCTURES....................................46

HEAD OF THE CHURCH ..................................................48

SECULAR WORLD.............................................................52

FULL TIME DILEMMA.......................................................54

HOW TO DO CHURCH .....................................................56

ABRAHAM VS MINISTRY PROMISE FULFILLED...............60

PASTOR'S FRATERNITY...................................................67

HOUSE CHURCH VS CHURCH MOVEMENT....................72

THE DNA OF THE CHURCH............................................77

## INTRODUCTION

One of the biggest things I have found is that often when we think of church, it brings different connotations into people's minds, often when they think about it, they think of a building, stain glass windows, structures, but I would like to just share some thoughts that I feel the Lord has given to me. One of the wonderful pictures about the church is that it is a **family**, it is a family of believers and one of the scriptures I like the most is

*"For this cause I bow my knees unto the Father of our Lord Jesus Christ of whom the whole family in heaven and earth is named that he would grant you according to the riches of his glory, to be strengthened with might by his Spirit in the inner man, that Christ may dwell in your hearts by faith; that ye, being rooted and grounded in love may be able to comprehend with all saints what is the breadth, and length, and depth, and height; and to know the love of Christ, which passeth knowledge, that ye might be filled with all the fullness of God. Now unto him that is able to do exceeding abundantly above all that we ask or think, according to the power that worketh in us, unto him be the glory in the church by Christ Jesus throughout all ages, world without end. Amen".*

**Ephesians 3:14-21(KJV)**

To me, one of the greatest things is love and God places us in families, it's the spirit of adoption, when the spirit of God adopts us to become one with him, there are many mysteries in the bible and when we talk about the mystery of Christ in us, we see that in Colossians, God wills us to know the richness of the glory of this mystery amongst the gentiles which is Christ in you the hope of glory.

*"To them God chose to make known how great among the Gentiles are the riches of the glory of this mystery, which is Christ in you, the hope of glory."*

**Colossians 1:27(ESV)**

So I found out that coming to know the Lord and His love was the key and foundation for everything, love is the greatest and perfect love casts out all fear, but what struck me as a Christian, as I came in and was brought in by friends into the church. There was such a variance within them, such a massive difference, I was questioning God about my early years, God how does this work? How should church work? The Lord began to speak to me particularly out of Mathew about the new wine skin.

*"No man putteth a piece of new cloth unto an old garment, for that which is put in to fill it up taketh from the garment, and the rent is made worst, neither do man put new wines into old bottles, else the bottles break, and the wine runneth out, and the bottles perish: but they put new wines into new bottles, and both are preserved".*

**Matthew 9:16-17(KJV)**

Having been brought up in a traditional church and then coming into a church where I saw the moving of the Holy Spirit, the power of God. I saw that people were literally looking to form the new wine skin, the ones that will hold the manifest presence of the Holy Spirit and the love of God. Then over a period of time began to watch some of these wine skins begin to tear and burst and I said God what is it, He took hold of my attention and He said "Ian I want you to wipe everything you have seen or thought about church and I want you to have a look at this scripture, it talks about how we are all to come together as a body, it talks about how

*"Eph 4:11 And he gave the apostles, the prophets, the evangelists, the pastor and teachers,*

*Eph 4:12 to equip the saints for the work of ministry, for building up the body of Christ,*

*Eph 4:13 until we all attain to the unity of the faith and of the knowledge of the Son of God, to mature manhood, to the*

*measure of the stature of the fullness of Christ,*

*Eph 4:14 so that we may no longer be children, tossed to and fro by the waves and carried about by every wind of doctrine, by human cunning, by craftiness in deceitful schemes.*

*Eph 4:15 Rather, speaking the truth in love, we are to grow up in every way into him who is the head, into Christ,*

*Eph 4:16 from whom the whole body, joined and held together by every joint with which it is equipped, when each part is working properly, makes the body grow so that it builds itself up in love."*

**Ephesians 4:11-13(ESV)**

I said to the Lord; as I have travelled around and been a Christian, I have seen some group of people, are "**prophets**", then they form groups, sometimes it is a church run by a **prophet**, he calls himself a "pastor" but he is actually a prophet. That is how a lot of prophetic people end up there.

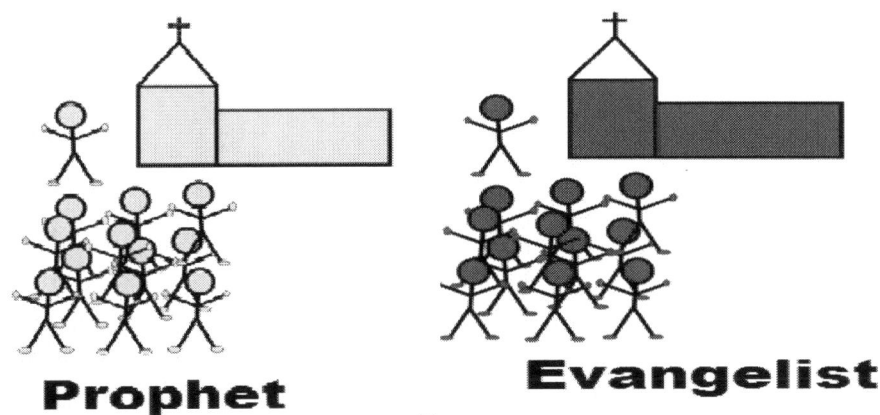

**Prophet**         **Evangelist**

There are some other groups; and the man that is running the group is an **"evangelist"**, so we have all these evangelists,

Then another group very solid in their teaching, so they have a **teaching** church,

**Teacher**          **Pastor**

Others that are counseling/ **pastors** and they have a **pastoral** church.

Why on earth are they not working together in one place? So I asked a few people and they told me, Ian that is the "Universal Church" bible scholars are saying that "they are not meant to be in one local church" and I was quite confused by that. I thought to myself, surely it will be much healthier if we had apostles, prophets, evangelists, pastors and teachers all working in the same place.

Surely if someone gets saved through the evangelist, it will be really helpful to have someone who can pastor them and someone who can disciple them as a teacher. Someone who is prophetic and can actually help clean the fish and could perhaps bring deliverance and words of knowledge and prophetic destiny into their lives. It would be incredibly helpful if we all are in the same place working together, that seems ideal but it doesn't seem to happen.

The tendency is uniformity, we see evangelists getting together, so we have school of evangelism. We have prophets getting together, so we have schools of prophets. We have teachers getting together, so we have bible schools or schools of training or teaching.

But a poor person like me who just got saved, the only way he can come to maturity and be equipped and trained will have to move from one camp to another, I will literally have to get saved through an evangelist and somehow find someone who will pastor me.

The trouble is if it's just a pastor running a church, then he is one man, he doesn't have the teachers or the prophets or apostles in his midst. Then I would have to roam around hoping to be brought to a place of maturity.

Who brings the people to maturity? I couldn't seem to get the right answer so I said, God help me?

He said Ian, the church is supposed to be a body, a building, a bride, he said Ian these are three key words and pictures that I give to the body of Christ to describe what the church is supposed to look like.

# THE BRIDE

The bride speaks of intimacy, speaks of marriage speaks of a commitment; God brings complete opposites and brings them together. If anyone has been married they know that if God wants to bring through unity, He is going to take people who are completely different and put them together.

So marriage is a wonderful picture in fact; Ephesians says

*"This mystery is profound, and I am saying that it refers to Christ and the church."*

**Ephesians 5:32 (ESV)**

So above that he talks about how the husband and wife leave their father and mother and become one, the two become one. He talks about how Christ is the head of the church and He is to serve and to love the body of Christ, husbands to love their wives, and wives to submit to their husbands, so I saw a wonderful picture of intimacy in the marriage. He said Ian; the marriage is one of the greatest mysteries in the bible, in fact it says the mystery is great, marriage is a great mystery, so the church is to be a picture of a bride.

In Genesis we have the marriage in the Garden of Eden.

*"Therefore a man shall leave his father and his mother and hold fast to his wife, and they shall become one flesh."*

**Genesis 2:24 (ESV)**

In Revelation 19 we find that Jesus is coming for His bride

*"Let us rejoice and exult and give him the glory, for the marriage of the Lamb has come, and his Bride has made herself ready;"*

**Revelation 19:7 (ESV)**

We find Abraham sends the servant to look for a bride for His son Isaac.

*"……but will go to my country and to my kindred, and take a wife for my son Isaac."*

**Genesis 24:4(ESV)**

The Father sends his servant to look, finds Rebecca and Rebecca comes back and they become one, here the Holy spirit has been sent by the heavenly Father to find a bride for his son Jesus.

Abraham as a Father of faith is the picture, Isaac and Rebecca, and what happens is that God is looking for a bride for his son, so I believe that the bride of Christ is an incredibly important revelation, to understand the marriage, intimacy of two complete opposites becoming one. Family is key, so we become sons and daughters of God, the next mystery after the bride which is riddled through the bible is the Body.

# THE BODY OF CHRIST

The Scripture we use is 1 Corinthians 12

*"For in one Spirit we were all baptized into one body—Jews or Greeks, slaves or free—and all were made to drink of one Spirit. For the body does not consist of one member but of many. If the foot should say, "Because I am not a hand, I do not belong to the body," that would not make it any less a part of the body. And if the ear should say, "Because I am not an eye, I do not belong to the body," that would not make it any less a part of the body. If the whole body were an eye, where would be the sense of hearing? If the whole body were an ear, where would be the sense of smell? But as it is, God arranged the members in the body, each one of them, as he chose. If all were a single member, where would the body be? As it is, there are many parts, yet one body. The eye cannot say to the hand, "I have no need of you," nor again the head to the feet, "I have no need of you." On the contrary, the parts of the body that seem to be weaker are indispensable, and on those parts of the body that we think less honourable we bestow the greater honour, and our unpresentable parts are treated with greater modesty, which our more presentable parts do not require. But God has so composed the body, giving greater honour to the part that lacked it, that there may be no division in the body, but that the members may have the same care for one another. If one*

*member suffers, all suffer together; if one member is honoured, all rejoice together. Now you are the body of Christ and individually members of it. And God has appointed in the church first apostles, second prophets, third teachers, then miracles, then gifts of healing, helping, administrating, and various kinds of tongues. Are all apostles? Are all prophets? Are all teachers? Do all work miracles? Do all possess gifts of healing? Do all speak with tongues? Do all interpret?"*

**1 Corinthians 12:13-30 (ESV)**

Here we find Paul very powerfully talking about the hand, the foot, the eye, the body, and then He intertwines that with the five fold in Ephesians 4, apostle, prophets and teachers, then I asked the Lord in a human body what will represent the teacher?

He said the brain, the mind,

I said what will represent the heart?

He said the pastor

I said what will represent the feet?

The evangelist

How blessed are the feet of those who bring the good news

I said what will represent the eye, mouth and ears?

The seers, the prophets, those who have ears to hear what the Spirit of God is saying.

I said it's quite fascinating that we have different parts of the body and the five fold, they have different functions they are gifts that Christ has given to the church. So we have the gifts of the Spirit

*"Now there are varieties of gifts, but the same Spirit; and there are varieties of service, but the same Lord; and there are varieties of activities, but it is the same God who empowers them all in everyone. To each is given the manifestation of the Spirit for the common good. For to one is given through the Spirit the utterance of wisdom, and to another the utterance of knowledge according to the same Spirit, to another faith by the same Spirit, to another gifts of healing by the one Spirit, to another the working of miracles, to another prophecy, to another the ability to distinguish between spirits, to another various kinds of tongues, to another the interpretation of tongues. All these are empowered by one and the same Spirit, who apportions to each one individually as he wills."*

**1 Corinthians 12:4-11 (ESV)**

Then you have offices, and people that are given, anyone can move in the gifts of the spirit, but the fact that you prophesy and move in the gift of prophecy doesn't make you a prophet, the fact that you have the word of knowledge or wisdom, doesn't make you a teacher, these are gifts of the spirit which is distributed by the spirit to all of us, gifts of healing and miracles, prophecy, tongues, interpretation of tongues etc. When it comes down to offices now the Lord is talking about the body. He says we are not all apostles, prophets or teachers; we are part of a body fitted together,

And I said to the Lord we often talk about the body of Christ? What does the body look like right now?

Instantly I saw an autopsy table, I saw the heart out of the chest sitting there, what struck me is that it was alive and pumping, I said Lord that is the heart? He said yes, I said how can it function without being attached to the body?

He said Ian I work all things for good for those who love me I can bring resurrection power even into that which is dead.

I said but it's not working with the other parts,

Then I saw the mind out the head, I can hear the mind saying can't you understand the word of God? Can't you divide the word? We are Berean's we help divide and understand the word of God. I thought fascinating, here is a brain operating and living without the rest of the body.

Then I saw feet running around the autopsy table cut off from the ankle, he said that is the evangelist. This helps to bring the good news, I'm called as an evangelist helping to preach the gospel. The feet running around doing his thing but completely separated from the body.

I said what a mess, he said the fact is that if we are not working together as a body, we are not a body, if we have prophets and they form schools of prophets then we are literarily just all eyes, we are not a body.

But Lord they say it's The Universal body, rather they are all there as the body of Christ but the lord said to me, this was written to the Corinthian church, this was a local church in a local city, he was not just talking to the whole church but Paul talking to them. Assuming the Corinthian church understood that there are apostles, prophets and teachers in the church, why would Paul write to them? Unless they were there in the church at Corinth, this is the opening letter to them, to the leaders.

People say I don't believe in the apostles and prophets, we have got the bible canonized that they don't even exist anymore. I found out that they still do because the bible said the gifts will pass away eventually, but when the perfect comes which is Christ in the second coming, for now we see in part and prophesy in part, then these things will not be needed because Christ will have fulfilled all of it.

*"For we know in part and we prophesy in part, but when the perfect comes, the partial will pass away. When I was a child, I spoke like a child, I thought like a child, I reasoned like a child. When I became a man, I gave up childish ways. For now we see in a mirror dimly, but then face to face. Now I know in part; then I shall know fully, even as I have been*

*fully known. So now faith, hope, and love abide, these three; but the greatest of these is love."*

**1 Corinthians 13:9-13(ESV)**


So I am absolutely convinced that we still have teachers, prophets and apostles here even in the body of Christ. When the bible was canonized it didn't eclipse the need for the office of a prophet or a pastor or teacher; in fact they are there to build up the body of Christ unto the unity of the faith, to equip them and to teach them.

# THE BUILDING

Then I say, God the body looks like it is very segregated and separated and I have seen that happen in different camps. He said "What you have identified is the problem" and I said God what is the next thing if we have heard the bride and the body. What is the next one? He said the bride of course is intimacy and the first love. Many have left their first love but the building gives structure,

- The bride gives intimacy
- The body gives function
- The building gives structure

You have heard people say 'me and Jesus, we are the church, if I find one other person and we agree in prayer, well, that is the church?' The Lord said 'No it is not!'

Let me show you clearly in the scripture what the building, the body of Christ looks like in structure.

*"For we are laborers together with God: ye are God's husbandry, ye are God's building. According to the grace of God which is given unto me, as a wise masterbuilder, I have laid the foundation, and another buildeth thereon. But let every man take heed how he buildeth thereupon. For other foundation can no man lay than that is laid, which is Jesus Christ. Now if any one build upon this foundation gold, silver,*

*precious stones, wood, hay, stubble; Every man's work shall be made manifest: for the day shall declare it, because it shall be revealed by fire; and the fire shall try every man's work of what sort it is. "*

**1 Corinthains 3:9-13 (KJV)**

Then we have the picture of the building that the Jews are trying to rebuild the temple, we see in Nehemiah the building of the temple and I understand that we are families. I said Lord teach me about the building and he said the building has foundations, walls, roof and complete structures. Let me unpack that for you, Ephesians 3, families and love, I then go on and talk about the Five Fold,

*"So then you are no longer strangers and aliens, but you are fellow citizens with the saints and members of the household of God, built on the foundation of the apostles and prophets, Christ Jesus himself being the cornerstone, in whom the whole structure, being joined together, grows into a holy temple in the Lord. In him you also are being built together into a dwelling place for God by the Spirit."*

**Ephesians 2:19-22 (ESV)**

It talks about the apostles and prophets being the foundation and Christ Jesus being the corner stone, when starting any building, the first thing you must do is put down a corner stone and Christ is the head of the body, head of the church, He is the corner stone. You don't have a building if you just have a cornerstone and I said that is obvious, often people say me and Jesus and someone else are standing on the cornerstone; "we are the church" He said no it's not; that is your relationship with me, Christ the rock of my salvation, Christ the cornerstone. Some of us have been called as prophets, as teachers building upon Jesus Christ the cornerstone. He said yes, but that is not the body of Christ, that is not the church and I said God help me.

The first thing you put down is the cornerstone, then the plumb line goes down and he said the stone in which the builders reject of course is Christ, the chief cornerstone. Many people build ministries and haven't got Christ the cornerstone.

Here I have the cornerstone, then next the foundation stones, the apostles and prophets, the scripture says in 1 Corinthians, apostles first and second prophets. And I said Lord when we have foundations laid, that is still not a building and he said the importance of getting the foundations laid, the apostolic and prophetic and it carries the weight of the building. Once that has been cured and once that has set,

**JESUS CHRIST THE CORNERSTONE WITH FOUNDATIONS OF PROPHETS AND APOSTLES**

the apostles and prophets working together, then I can now put what they call a bottom plate, then we can start to build.

I said who will be the next and He said the walls are the teachers. They put the parameter and the word of God to form the living room, dinning, kitchen, bathroom and different parts of the building or house; up go the walls, the interior, and the support.

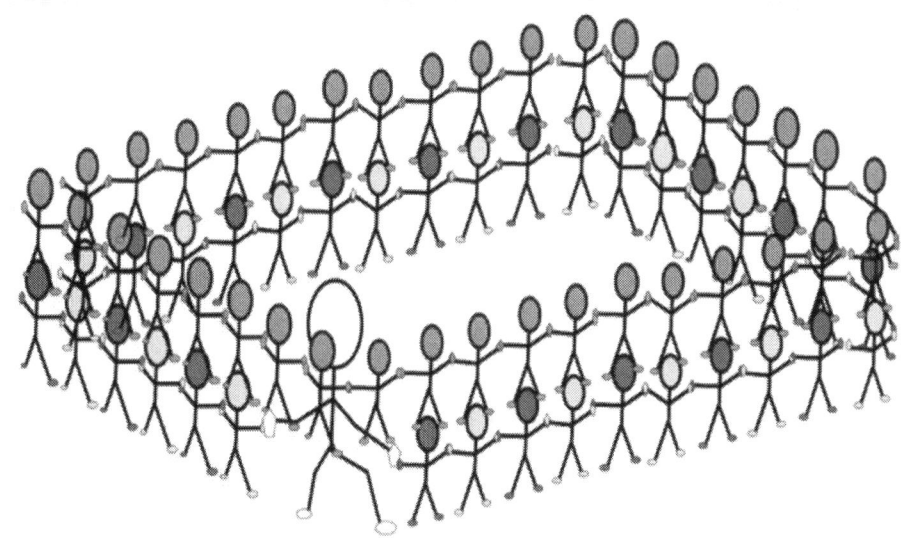

JESUS CHRIST THE CORNERSTONE WITH FOUNDATIONS OF PROPHETS AND APOSTLES SHOWING TEACHERS AS THE WALLS

The next thing is the roof; I said what is that He said the Pastor, the covering. He said firstly, Christ the cornerstone, then apostles and prophets, then teachers.

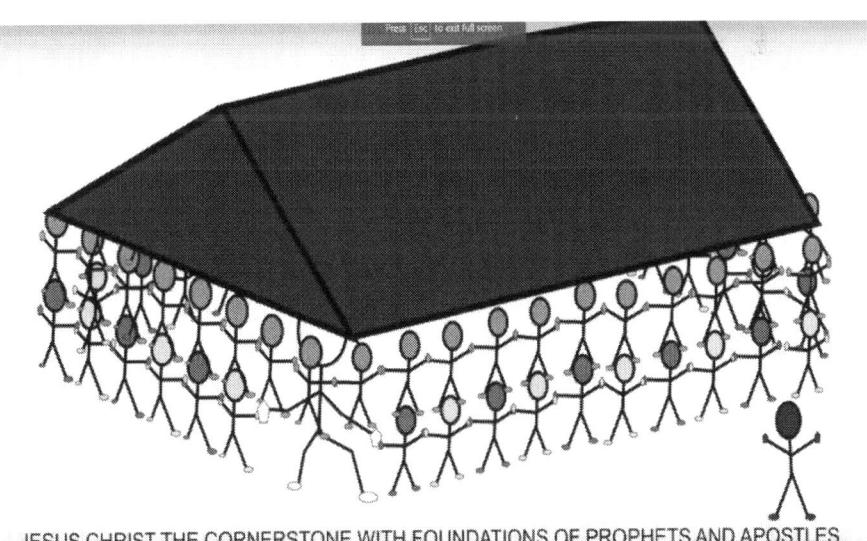

JESUS CHRIST THE CORNERSTONE WITH FOUNDATIONS OF PROPHETS AND APOSTLES SHOWING TEACHERS AS THE WALLS, AND THE PASTOR AS THE ROOF

And I said what next, and he said then of course we then have the evangelists who bring the living stones to fit into the house. Then the building becomes the church.

THE EVANGELISTS BRING IN THE NEW CHRISTIANS

Then I asked how does the ministry of hospitality, helps and mercy work for them? In Romans 12, Paul talks about how the ministries helps, hospitality and the ministration of gifts turn it from a house or building into a home, they bring in furniture, then turn it into a living home.

*"For the perfecting of the saints, for the work of the ministry, for the edifying of the body of Christ"*

**Ephesians 4:12 (KJV)**

Joined together with the Romans 12 to form the house of the lord, a family, a community, a place where love is the key, is all bound together, unity in diversity, one church, one body, one bride. The picture of unity comes together here with all of the gifts which are different but working together.

It sounds wonderful, so what happens? Then he said the Glory of God fills the house and we represent Christ in his full nature so, when you look at the different aspect of who Christ is, you stand to see that it reflects the true church and they are to take on principalities and powers and that is another mystery. The declaration against principalities and powers in heavenly places is to come through the church. And I say lord what does the building look like right now; we have got the bride, the body in which I have dis-membered.

What does the building looks like?

Instantly in an open vision, I saw a roof on the ground and the cornerstone holding the roof top literally lying off the ground, I watched people walk up to the roof, lift the roof up and climb underneath it

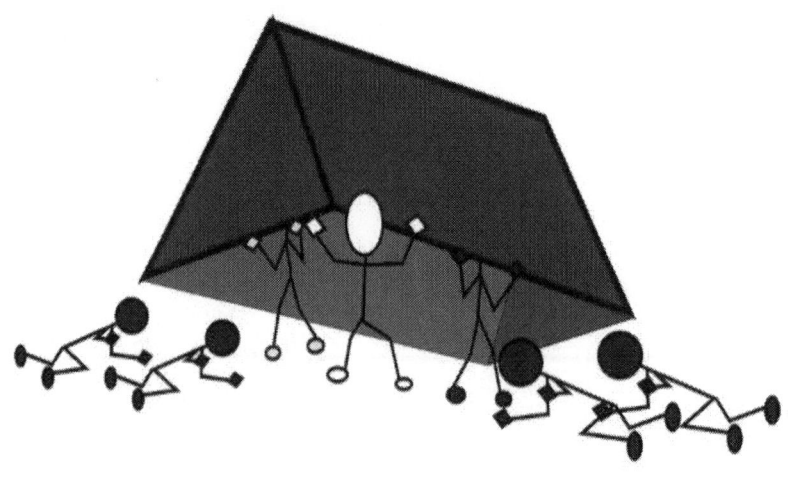

**JESUS CHRIST THE CORNERSTONE SUPPORTING THE ROOF AND PEOPLE LIFTING IT**

And I said what is that?

He said Ian that is the pastor; the roof, the covering, for the people to come under the covering they have to be very low to the ground and because of this Christ the cornerstone is holding a small light shining into the covering.

In the vision, I turn to my left and I saw foundation stones literally just above the ground and rebar rods coming out. Have you seen a building site that had to stop for some reason possibly due to money, they have not been able to finish and I said yes. I said all the foundations look solid and you can hardly see them and He said those are apostles and prophets who are so deep into me, hidden in me they are barely visible to the naked eye and they are so low to the ground in humility, no one wants to work with them.

I then looked between the foundation and the ground on the roof and saw in the distance, a young man standing on a rock in a field with 200 people listening to him, as I heard him preaching the gospel, 'repent the kingdom of heaven is at hand, Christ has called you!' And I was thinking what is that? He said that was an evangelist having an open air, I have seen that too.

If you ask the evangelist, he will say I have been called by God to evangelize, he will say I am not called to pastor, I am not called to prophesy, I am called to evangelize. Here he is preaching to people in an open air, how do they get discipled? Who is going to teach them? Who is going to pastor them?

I have seen this, the poor pastor running the church, the evangelist is running his crusade, the prophets, running their own school of prophetic ministry and we have got absolute, complete separation of the Five Fold, none of them working together.

Again in the vision, I saw a building, a window, a house, it looked like a complete house, a roof and people walking into it and said God is that the church? He said I don't want you to look into it and I said can I go into the vision and then saw hundreds of people worshipping God and I began to lift my hand in worship.

Then God said don't look up, look down, as I looked down, He said what do you see? I said I see dirt, I see earth. And he said what do you see in this building? I said I see walls, teachers, a roof, a pastor, an evangelist, he brought in souls but when I look down I see there is no foundation with scripture or apostles and prophets. There is no prophetic, apostolic leadership, and as I look carefully I can see the cornerstone and if you asked the people what is the basis of this ministry?

We build this church on Christ, we have a pastor, a teacher, a youth evangelist and we have 3 out of the five fold. Then I said God what happened? And He said so many churches have not got apostolic and prophetic foundations.

Ask the master builder in the church, if you found a building that has no foundation, what will you do? He said son, scrap it and start again. He said it is crazy to lift the building up and put a new foundation.

He said do you think many churches will shut down their ministry to restart with prophets and apostles and rebuild?

I said no,

He said Ian am going to send an earthquake through the body of Christ, what will be shaken will be shaken. He said judgment starts first in the house of God, he said my desire is to build the body of Christ, the bride, there is structure, there is intimacy and there is love.

Until we get the blue print of what the bible talks about, we will continue to build haphazardly not as master builders but as foolish builders.

# YEARS OF MINISTRY

What I began to realize is that I have travelled around for nearly 32 years in ministry. I end up in refugee camps with people who are offering mercy ministries to refugees coming out of war torn countries. I often see their compassion, giving clothing, digging wells, but if you want to evangelize or prophecy to them, you will be chased out because you will be told not to upset what they are doing. I was finding we have uniformity, mercy ministry people have formed their own groups.

When I move into other camps, there will be open heavens, angels, the voice of God, access to the throne room and seeing Christ in the heavenly realm. I have been taken by the Lord into these realms, they will be in spiritual warfare and opening up wells and again there was uniformity a stack of prophets.

Then you move into another camps and here comes the evangelist, they say: save the lost, get out into the high ways and by ways and bring them in! What I found again is uniformity; birds of a feather flock together, a stack of evangelists; if you decide to teach about discipleship or teach other things that are needed to clothe and feed them. They would always look at you sideways, saying this is not what we are called to do; we are called to save them.

I began speaking to another group called teachers, saying most of the evangelistic crusades that are done, only 1% of them end up in the church. We can go out there and get all of them saved, but we have to disciple them and bring them up with the word, if not we will never see them come through.

Then I began to realize that, we were doing evangelism in the street and leading 3000 people to the lord with signs, wonders and miracles, and one day God told me, where are they? You have prayed for these people, you have led them into supernatural encounters; the divine, called treasure hunts etc. Then God said where are they? I was shocked and said that is right.

Bringing all these people in through the evangelist, but the problem is they are spiritual babies, they are born again in a park, on a train, shopping centers, the question is, were they transitioning into the body of Christ?

Of course they were not. We are doing the work of the evangelist and we are moving in power but none of them were coming through to be part of a family, a community and fitting together into the body of Christ. When we bring them into the house, we were giving lists and names, we have no relationship with their church, we are not even part of their church and the church was run by one man called a pastor, because that is how the old wine skin functioned. This poor guy cannot even look after the people he had, let alone disciple the 100's of people been saved on the street,

Then the Lord said Ian, your fruit will not remain if you continue doing this. So I stopped! I literarily stopped in my tracts, and tried to speak to the evangelists on how they should be connected with pastors and teachers, I got the same old reaction of "that is not what we are called to do." We are called into the ministry to save souls, we are not into pastoring, teaching or discipleship that is not our job. If you don't connect with the other guys you will find your fruit fall to the ground.

Then I went around the teachers, they were saying "we are to form bible schools and run seminars" and I said you have no clue about pastoring anybody, I said you will give a 5 point sermon on how to sort your life out, when they actually need pastors and evangelists, you don't get anybody to teach, if you don't get anyone saved.

I saw this bizarre situation where you have different camps, throwing stones at each other. None of them agree and all of them moving into a smaller hole called uniformity. So I realized that the church was left to run by a man called the pastor. Mentioned once in the bible in Ephesians 4:11, he tries to get anyone to help him, well all his teachers have gone to bible schools, all his evangelists have gone off to crusades somewhere and all the prophets have run away to form the school of prophets.

So one group will say you are not giving me any scope in your church cause it was run by one man and you don't have any revelation of my calling or gifting, then we decide to form other groups.

There were business man doing dinners and people who formed women's groups that became Glo groups. I have moved around all these camps and I found they were not the church, they would say "we go to a church but we are not the church, we are helping doing the work of the ministry." I tell them actually you are! I say why don't you join it, well they won't let me because that structure won't allow me to come in and help minister, the only way I can grow up using my gift is to come out into this Para church organization. To grow in my maturity and my gifting, so I saw the same disintegration of unity, I saw complete disunity, I began to find the only unity they had was uniformity.

They all thought the same, all were wounded, all were hurt, they all formed their own little camps and I say don't want anything to do with church, don't talk to me about the church, I will just do God calling, that is my ministry. Don't stop me doing my ministry, I am helping the church by doing what I am doing out here. And I asked do you have any relationship? You go to church but when it comes to authority who do you submit to, they said I submit to the leadership team and I have set up in my own camp.

What a complete mess…….

We have got people getting saved over here but nowhere to take them, because the people who have saved them have no relationship with their community and the reason why is that its run by one man, and the pastor is saying where is my youth evangelist?

They are all gone! Where are my people that are teaching the disciples? They are all gone! Where are my prophets? Well I don't even believe in them, they are gone over there and are slightly weird! So the poor guy keeps running the church by himself.

So we have multitude of ministry mushrooming out, everything based around gifting and calling but none of them understanding that leaders in which Christ has called also are supposed to work in the same place. If they were, they will have to work together and I say Lord is not as if there is the problem with the sheep but the leaders and He said that is right, it is a new wineskin.

# THE HAND

The whole basis of unity, is unity and diversity, He said look at your hand and what did you see, I said five

I said who is the apostle?

**The thumb:** He can do everything, he can prophecy, he can evangelize, he can pastor and he can teach.

**The Index finger**: The prophet, apostles and prophets are supposed to work together in the foundation of the church.

**The Middle finger:** Evangelist great signs and wonders.

**The Ring finger:** The pastor.

**The Pinky**: the teacher, the small one who could get into small places to divide the word accurately, the Bearean.

He said you try and get the prophet to work with the teacher, I say very difficult. You try to get the evangelist to work with a teacher, you try to get the pastor and teacher that can work along each other, the pastor and the evangelist can work alongside each other.

Often you have a pastor, teacher and evangelist working together seemingly, often have a youth pastor who has been employed as an evangelist, and he is the 3rd in the string, a pastor, a teacher, and evangelist. Then often if the youth pastor gets too big, insecurity comes then the youth pastor has to leave and form a ministry or start his own group of church.

The problem of course is that prophets and apostles are not even recognized do not even exist in some of these denominations or people in the body of Christ and I said Lord, of all these different giftings, how does it work? With all the prophets, the seers or the schools of prophets, what you do is poking the devil, if you are in the school of evangelism, uniformity, you bring lost people to be saved, but you won't be getting them pastored, discipled and cleaned-up. If you are left running a church, you will be absolutely frustrated because anybody you raised up is actually going to leave, is going to leave to join these other camps because you are running it by yourself.

And the teacher will say, we are the ones that know the bible, so we are the ones that come through intellectually, through the bible school and then everyone must pass through us, the teacher. The bible says the first is the apostle, second prophets and third the teachers.

We have relegated intellectualism to be the basis of revelation of God's knowledge, not by the Spirit half the time but by understanding the word intellectually. The bible says we are not to do that, but then we get this theological and intellectual basis of teaching around the so called knowledge of the word, but we are not getting it by revelation or by insight.

I said Lord what does each one of these groups then reproduce? Prophets will reproduce schools of prophets, evangelists will reproduce crusades and schools of evangelism, pastor then trying to reproduce the church, but they are not the church because they are missing 4 out of the five fold, then we get guys reproducing bible schools. Some have gone out and say we are on a mission, what kind of mission are you into? We are missionaries; we are going out to the lost of the world. So I join the camps of the prophets, what do you guys doing? We go out to binding strong men, principalities and power, opening up wells, and we are going out in spiritual warfare and calling on angels to come on the place, I ask them who are you working with? They say that is what we are doing! And to the evangelist, what are you guys doing? We go to crusades, we get people saved, we go to the streets and we get masses of people giving their hands up for Jesus Christ. And I said who did you work with? No one really, we have local church to join in our crusade.

And I asked how many people are get into the church, and I say my bible school teacher says about 1% and I said do you really want to change how you do it? Oh no, they are saved, there are signs and wonders and miracles and I go on to the pastors, what are you guys doing? We are planting churches! I say just the same as you got back in the West? Ones that are missing everything else? Then I go to the teachers what are you guys doing? We are training leaders to actually take over the church and I said that is unbelievable.

Then we got the romans 12 hospitality, mercy ministries, they got so sick of the fivefold not working together that they have set up mercy ministries, feeding the hungry, opening wells, hospitals, orphanages, so the administrators, compassionate ministries, say these guys (the five fold) don't know what they are doing, they have set up their own camps and when it comes to evangelizing and prophesy and making it into churches, they say that is not what we are called to do. Well we are called to do mercy, feeding those in the hospitals.

## THE PUZZLE

To the different camps I went to, they all have a part of the puzzle, you know how you have a puzzle and different parts of it are supposed to make a whole puzzle. What was striking me and was frustrating me, was that each of them had truth, each one of them was the call of God, each of them was bringing the part of the mystery of God, compassion, healing, visiting the hospitals, visiting the prisons, but the problem was there was no connection and if they did get anyone saved, how they will connect with the rest of the body?

None of them were being brought to maturity and the poor people have to walk around like lost sheep, trying to see how they can come to the fullness of the knowledge of Christ. And I said God this can be quite frustrating!

I said how does the apostle work? He said the apostle can prophecy, he can evangelize, he can pastor and he can teach. He said the job of the apostle is like a chameleon, he can literally change color, he can see eye to eye with other ministries, his job is to get these 4 guys who set up their own little ministry camps to actually work together in one place. And form a new wineskin called the bride, the building, the body, but apart from revelation by the Holy Spirit of the passage in Ephesian 4, they will never see it.

The danger is, if your ministry becomes your identity and what you do for Christ is your meaning and purpose, you will lose the understanding, that the mystery **is Christ in you**, not what you do. If you ministry becomes your baby, your husband or your wife, then that becomes your purpose.

If you understand that the roles of those ministries you are called to, being called as an evangelist or a prophet is to work together with the others. Why? For the working up of the body of Christ in love, submitting to one another in love, maintaining unity.

If you try to get all the pastors together you have unity, if you have all the church working together? The Sheep are screaming this out "please churches work together", ministries work together. But the reality is that they won't because each one of them has their own little impact, their own little ministries. If they would work together, they have to work together in the same place and in one place; it's called a local church.

## OLD TESTAMENT STRUCTURES

People say I don't believe you need apostles in a local church and I said, look you can be an apostle 1000's, 100's, or 10's. In the Old Testament Moses was given this by Jethro, by God to Moses, How? Instead of doing it all yourself, to delegate to captains of a 1000, if you are in a small community, you can go to a local church having an apostle captain of 10, teachers in 10, prophets in 10, evangelists in 10.

If we have five of the fivefold or leaders working in the same place, you will honestly have a church that grows to 50 people, that could be half the community in some of those small villages, so why not have apostles of 10 if you are in a mega city like London, of course you need to be an apostle of 1,000's because there are millions of people to be saved. If you have five, then at least you have 5,000 members of the church, if you have apostles of a 1,000 then you work together, the potential of the church is growing instead of just growing it yourself.

If you are a prophet and you try to grow a church, do you know what you going to do? You are most likely going to get frustrated with the lack of holiness in a life of black and white and this may likely cause decrease in the local church because they will never be good enough.

If you are an evangelist, you will get a lot of people saved; your church will have so much turnover of growth. You will be filling everyone else's church but you can't pastor them.

If you are a pastor, you can't seem to evangelize to anybody except when you hire a good itinerate until then you most likely won't get much church growth.

If you are a teacher, you may have your sermon with people flooding out of churches that are not being taught, are being saved but not discipled, you may end up with the guys that are running evangelistic churches or pastoral churches that are not being taught the word. They may all gravitate to you but they may not stay there long because one day they might think that there is more of the Spirit elsewhere and end up with a group of prophets or apostolic people. Who may show them that there is a greater knowledge of who God is!

# THE HEAD OF THE CHURCH

Each one of us have part of the puzzle, if we think we have got the full revelation of Christ, we will then camp around it, if we realized that

Jesus is the apostle,

Jesus is the prophet,

Jesus is the evangelist,

Jesus is the teacher,

Jesus is the pastor,

He is the apostle of our faith, the spirit of prophecy is upon Him Revelation 19:10, He is the shepherd looking for the lost sheep, the evangelist: He is the shepherd of our souls that walks through the valley and the shadow; He is the pastor who came comfort, to heal, to hold and to be our friend. He is also the teacher, so Christ himself, all the gifts; all the offices are in him. Do you know that Jesus was smart enough not to give it all to the one person? If He gives to one person and calls him a pastor, what has he got? The fullness of the revelation of Christ to one individual.

What we have got is a very dangerous situation, we have got one individual who thinks he is going to equip and train, because he realized quickly he can't, he ends up hiring an evangelist or a teacher and there is a massive rotating individual ministry going around continually on the road as a hireling.

They are not part of the community; they are not part of that particular group. I have no problem with cross-pollination but we have got an exceeding mess of ministries revolving around a local church run by one individual. If he is the fullness of who Christ is, then he will equip and train them.

The fact is Christ says I have given these people to the church, if these people are not being recognized, you know what happens, they will be frustrated by the fact that it was run by one person. They then go out and find, and gravitate to people who have got the same gifting as them and are driven out of what is called the existing body of Christ. Those people who run the church say they are a Para church, the reality is their church if it is run by a one man bands are paraplegic themselves.

I said God what happens if we then get the apostles, who employ them, the apostles still becomes the head but He said Ian what you then have is a clubbed hand, he gives responsibility but the authority has not been delegated. You end up with a super apostle who then employs evangelists, pastors and teachers because he knows this. He then starts a corporate type structure with a flow diagram and He is the head of it. I said who is supposed to be the Head and He says I am the Head, not the apostles. And I said what the people say first is the apostles, based upon the scripture and second prophets, and he said that is not positional; the greatest leader must be the greatest servant.

So the whole key to understanding 1 Corinthians 12: Says apostles must be the greatest servant and the greatest one who will lay their life down, if he controls and dominates it, he will lord over them like the they do in a corporate structure, he understands what needs to be done and he becomes the boss. And I said who is supposed to be the head of the church, the apostle, the bishops; He said Christ is the head. I said that makes such sense.

He said it is not singular, it is plural, in the Corinthian church when they have the word of prophesy, they make sure two or three other prophets check it out, when you have one prophet, that prophet can be taken out, when a church has one apostle, he can make a mistake, when you have one evangelist etc.

He said I have given evangelists, prophets and apostles, to the church. If you understand this to be a local church and not a theological universal church, then you understand Ephesians much better.

When you spend many years ministering in all the different groups and all the different camps, you get a little bit cynical or think how can we fix this? I see the problem, how do we fix it? Paul wrote what is called the Ephesians, in fact the original manuscript does not have Ephesus, many scholars believed it was a circulatory letter sent to all churches.

When you get older, perhaps you have seen a lot of what has happened and beginning to gain understanding on how to form a new **wineskin.** How to bring the body, the bride, the building into foremost, he then begins to speak, Christ has given these to the church, if we accept it, it is not a letter to all the churches but to Ephesus. Then Ephesian church had apostles, prophets, pastors, teachers and evangelists, Paul was talking how they must work together in unity.

In the book of Acts, we find out there are 12 apostles in the early church, like always man is always trying to find who is the head apostle, who is the big boss, some will say it is James, some will say Peter, who is the head of the Jerusalem church? Paul addresses them and says I am not a follower of Peter, I am not the follower of James, I am a follower of Jesus. The danger is when we start putting the apostles, teachers, pastors, or putting someone above anyone else, we end up with a pyramid structure. Christ is the head. The best thing for mankind to do is to walk together in humility and the biggest difficulty is for leaders to work together not the Sheep but Shepherds.

# THE SECULAR WORLD

The leaders in which Christ has given, half of the time we drive these people out of the church, not that this is premeditated but by default they end up walking in the world. So we end and say "We have got no leaders," but they are very busy working, we have apostles running companies, as CEO, we have prophets bringing inventions, we have evangelists running sales teams and we have public relations officers paying our people, and Human Resources who are pastors involved in major companies. We have teachers who are accountants and lawyers, then we have a bizarre situation.

I am called to the church and I am called to the world, so we have apostles in the business world and in the church. We have this understanding that there are potentially apostles in both, that is a new revelation. Now we are trying to separate the two, the church and the world and I asked God how does that work? It doesn't, if you are a true apostle in the call, then it is not in or out, it is not one or the other. If you understand that you are an apostle and you understand that you have a leadership team of apostles, and prophets, and pastors and teachers running the church not a professional one man band, so we can have 90% of our leadership working in a single job. We can have men and women who are actually working in the cold face of the real world and helping lead the church in an eldership.

They will be representing the fivefold, one said to me, I know that I am called to be an apostle but am running a corporation, how can I transition and be part of a local church government as an apostolic person. What they want from me is my money because I am a business man, they don't want me to lead in the church, they want me to finance the leaders in the church.

And I said sir, if I ask you how many times you could preach and really lead, I said 3 or 4 times and you still run businesses and I said what if we have 12 leaders representing the fivefold just to say and you have 3 or 4 times to preach throughout the year, could you be partly full time in your work and still carry the weight of the leadership instead of a one man band, you won't be running the church but would be part of the leadership representing the fivefold and he said I can do that, I have never heard that.

I said guess what, we get people saved, we like to give them jobs and it will be really good for you to keep your day job, we know you are an apostle and in the new wineskin, we will give you an opportunity to lead, and to preach as a teaching elder, a prophet and an evangelist. Salesman, men who are in the workforce can be part of that leadership, in the new wineskin they can be part of that government.

## THE FULL TIME DILEMMA

The problem is we have got this professionalism, that I can only be truly be a man of God if I go full time. So if we have got this ministry, I must go full time. We have all these poor people leaving their jobs, leaving their university degree, jumping out to go to bible schools, to go full time because you must go through bible school to become a full time minister.

We have got practical camps, going to the school of ministry, school of supernatural, school of something. The danger is since they are going to leave their jobs, their university degrees, leaving any form of education. If they spend 2 or 3 years in the bible school or training center and then try to re-enter the workforce, you know what is going to happen, once you have finished your course, what does your C.V look like.

Any employer in the real world is going to look at that, and say you have been away for 4 years out of the workforce, what do you want to do now? I would like to work? How long are you going to work here for? Until God calls me because my real call is to be an evangelist and to save nations but I need to pay my bills, to pay my rent right now and that has not come to pass yet, and the guy looks at you and says sorry but, I need someone who is committed for a career, a lifetime in business. How then will I put you in charge?

One day God spoke to me and when you are gone, he may not even voice this out, but that is why you don't get the job. Then we have seen thousands of young kids living with the hope that maybe they will be put into full time positions. The frustration is that a lot of these kids have destroyed their potential to be in the work force.

I have seen terrible advice given to young kids, when people come to our church in London, I say keep your day job, finish your degree, get a job. If you want to change the world and influence the nations, we can in a new wineskin, you get to preach, we can get you to grow into maturity here in this local church, if we see the gifting and calling, you can come into it and assume your leadership position in the five fold. You can start to take your role as an evangelist, or a pastor or a teacher.

The key thing that God wanted us to do is the new wineskin. He wanted us to understand that He can only help by revelation. You have got a problem before you look for the solution, I believe God has given us solutions through the fivefold and I pray that somehow within your spirit you will grab hold of it and you will begin to ask God, show me the revelation of the body, the bride, the church in Jesus name.

## HOW TO DO CHURCH

I will share this as best as I can, something of the revelation God has given me on how to do church, the big one I found as we began to try and do this is that often you try to learn what not to do before you find out what you should be doing. Most of us have learnt the hard way, throughout the book of Acts, we find Paul trying to figure out how to do church, he gets saved on the Damascus road, he tries to work with the existing apostles has difficulty, Barnabas the son of encouragement picks him up. We find him falling out with other prophets, falling out with Barnabas, other apostles, we see him doing 2 years of Teranus bible school, he tried everything, a one man band, a team...... he tried everything.

When you look at the book of Acts, you can justify any ministry, from deliverance, to evangelism, to teaching. You can try anything you like, but the book of acts does not give us a blueprint for how to do church. Paul begins to write Ephesians, the epistles, he hadn't tried everything. In fact he often goes back and find out in his missionary journeys how on earth it is working, he had up to 45 co-workers, but we think it is Paul, but it was never Paul, it was a team. He began to realize the need for each other, he began to realize the need for the fivefold. And of course we have one of the least of the apostles Barnabas, who was the son of encouragement pick up one of the imminent apostles. We then find of course the Antioch church is wonderful and very interesting, as it says

*"There was a great persecution against the church which was at Jerusalem; and they were all scattered abroad throughout the regions of Judaea and Samaria, except the apostles".*

**Acts 8:1-5 (ESV)**

So you now found out that God wanted the Jerusalem church to begin to expand, to literally reach the world. The apostles didn't leave they became very comfortable, you find in Acts 8 everyone went except the apostles. We found in Acts 13 the people that were scattered out from Jerusalem with no name, no face, some of them ended up in Antioch. Then major apostles in other parts of the church that were scattered from the persecution were in Antioch, we find out that there are prophets and teachers, Barnabas, Simon.

There we find Paul and Barnabas turn up, so these churches were not formed by Paul, the apostles or Barnabas, but were literally started by people scattered out of the Jerusalem church. They realized that there are not super-apostles, they were not the 12, they were not the ones that were discipled by Christ for 3 years, so they must have realized the need to work together. So often when you don't have a name or ministry, you then become a little bit more humble to say perhaps you don't have the full revelation of Christ, so I need to work with other people. In the Antioch church which has become the center of the world mission of the church and the planting of churches, it is made up of a bunch of no name, no face people scattered.

So I say young apostles, young prophets, young teachers, who were scattered out of Jerusalem, some of them ended up in Antioch and they formed one of the largest churches known to the world and it eclipsed the Jerusalem church. The Holy Spirit leads Paul and Barnabas to it, what they are doing, they watch, they learn, they were actually blown away with what they see. Theatres filled, souls being saved, and then we find the Holy Spirit that these men enjoy there on the leadership team in Antioch and the church has prophets on staff.

I have seen a lot of churches that don't believe in Prophets. Here we also have teachers on staff who are not only running bible schools, we know that people are been saved so there have to be evangelists, we know that the bible says it's a church, so there are pastors. I thought to myself what an extra-ordinary thing, when we have apostles, prophets, pastors, teachers and evangelists here and God begins to use this as the sending base for Paul and Barnabas. I was so excited because it was a new wineskin, a whole new church.

Often God uses persecution to scatter us up because He is not getting our ear. He told the apostles to go to Judaea, Samaria, and the uppermost parts of the earth. The danger when we don't do what God has asked us to do, God sometimes gives us a bit of a move on, or a bit of shake-up

## ABRAHAM VS MINISTRY PROMISE FULFILLED

I've found a lot of people that have been pushed out of the existing wineskin, have difficulty not being recognized and released in the church. Once they have got their ministry, once they have got their promise, once they have got the fulfillment of what they wanted to do, it is very hard to let them go. It is like a monkey putting his hand to a cage, grabbing peanuts and he won't let it go. So I found a wonderful picture of the promise being fulfilled through Abraham, the father of faith. He was promised a son, he was given Isaac and one day, God said once he got the promise, to take that promise, take the fulfillment and take it to a mountain, and said I want you to kill it.

For most people, their promise or the fulfillment of their promise becomes their baby, becomes their answer to prayer. You know what the Lord often does? Do not look at the promise even though it's fulfilled, be willing to literally kill it.

I found that God gave me a ministry and the danger was that the ministry becomes the focus, I have fulfilled my ministry, I am hearing so much about your destiny, your ministry, your calling, that is right, you have destiny, you have a calling. When you are called out of a structure like this, the frustration is that it is only you, one person who has got the calling and is full-time, the rest are not released.

When you get to fly, when you do get to fulfill your destiny, the problem is you hold on to it so tightly, it becomes the purpose, if anyone tries to stop it, you see it as a threat, and you will eventually try to take anyone out who wants to stop you from fulfilling your ministry. You think it's demonic and it might be God actually telling you to put a knife to that ministry and make sure it has not become your purpose, your baby, your wife.

I meet some who people say don't you dare take my ministry away? What if you have no ministry? I'm called to....., "they say", well you may be called to..... but is your identity in what you do for Christ? Or is your identity in Him? If you are secure in him, Christ alone, your ministry is not your focus but He is, Jesus. The Bible says fix your eyes on Jesus, he didn't say fix your eye on your calling, gifting, ministry or what you are going to do for Christ.

When I died and went to heaven, what struck me was that I had done nothing but pray the sinner's prayer in an ambulance, the Lord's Prayer, and I am now standing before the king of glory, seeing his manifest presence and He is loving me, filling me with love and acceptance, Holiness and purity. I was weeping like a child when I came back to earth and God called me to go into ministry and to preach, I then realized that nothing I did for them in the way of ministry, saving souls, praying for the sick, leading people to the knowledge of Christ, would that increase His loving hand for me?

*"For whoever has entered God's rest has also rested from his works as God did from his. Let us therefore strive to enter that rest, so that no one may fall by the same sort of disobedience."*

**Hebrews 4:10-11 (ESV)**

The obedient enter the rest, cease from your own works, stop striving, so many of us have strived because we have been frustrated and not been able to minister. The trouble is when you do get a chance to minister in or outside the body of Christ, the danger is it becomes your focus. If you become so focused on the ministry, it can actually burn you out.

I found out that when we come into the knowledge of the rest of God, then you are not fighting for your ministry, what you are actually doing is you are fighting to see the body of Christ become a bride. You are trying to get the heart of Christ, what does He want? A pure and holy bride, a body that work together in unity, love, a building that represents the house of the Lord that has structure, that has form. If it's just about you and Jesus and your ministry, you will very quickly become separated from your body, very quickly separated from the blueprints of the church and then you will be fighting to keep your ministry.

## Ministry and Money

In fact in these days, if you do not have the understanding of how you can be in full time work and have a ministry, you will have literally created a ministry where the ministry has to feed you.

All good and well when you are single and can travel around the world, but when you are married, certainly there comes stability and settling, when you have children there comes a stability. So if you are an itinerate prophet, an itinerate evangelist or an itinerate teacher, guess what? The only position that provides any form of stability, any form of income is going to be a pastor.

Then if you are not called to be a pastor, you are going to have real issues because the existing wineskin only provides pastoral positions maybe youth evangelism, maybe an associate as a teacher but literally you are going to find your ministry is supporting you, your ministry becomes your funding, do you understand what am saying? I am talking to people that are in ministry.

What we have got is a serious situation, we have got when the ministry becomes a means to an end. The danger is that the itinerates then say "the church doesn't look after me, so I will have to charge them", they will have to pay a fee, I will have to sell something, I have to get people to support me. So instead of the tithe going into the house, the tithe goes to all these itinerate ministries.

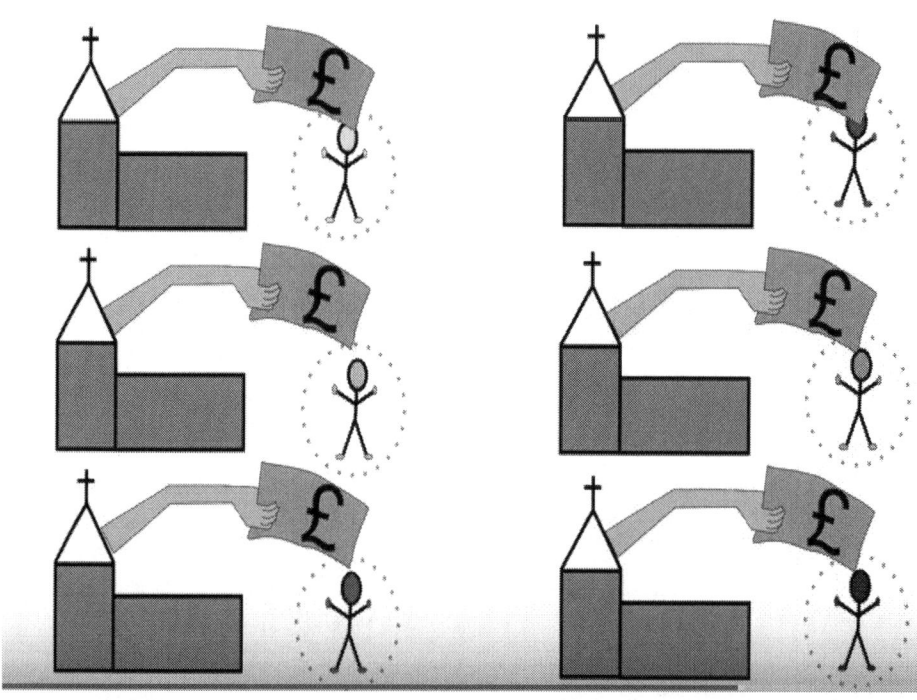

I have got a prophetic ministry, so I want you to tithe to me, I am your source of revelation and I am not a church but I need part of the tithe. Instead of gathering it into the store house, which is the house, the house of the Lord, the building, which should be on staff, because you are not on staff like the Antioch church. Prophets are not on staff, teachers are not on staff, apostles are not on staff, what ends up happening is that these people need to have an income and so they end up itinerating.

Some don't want to itinerate so they say; you come to my school evangelism, you come to my school of prophetic ministry. I can't be bothered travelling around the world, but if you want to be trained and taught, you come to me so you pay for the training. I got it freely but you have got to be paying me to be taught. If you want to be my intern, you must pay a fee. I have seen this kind of stuff going on in proliferation, so each person is desperately trying to maintain their ministry.

Each one of these ministries becomes a charitable trust and needs to be funded. Then we have got 15,000 different Ministries out there calling out for money because of course, they are doing the work of the Lord. We have a deliverance ministry, therefore we need funding. Church doesn't do deliverance, we do, we are the experts, we need you to fund us, you will have to leave the church and come to us. We are the ones to teach you, we will give you the knowledge of the word of God, they don't disciple, they don't teach you properly, you don't need to go to their bible school, you can come and I will teach you and I will do the course, the long term course, the short term course, I am the teacher, you come along to my bible school because I have one.

Also we have the evangelist, you will have to come to my school of evangelism, you will have to pay a fee to do that because actually I have to put food on my table and feed my family. In fact am building more and more, my ministry is bigger than the local church, mine is a global ministry, so I need to get a bigger part of the pie. So we have the money going out to a million different Para church ministries, none of them bringing unity, none of them bringing anything but uniformity, all of them separating the money out of the house of the Lord.

Instead of saying you can keep your day job, you can work, we can equip and train you here in the local body as the fivefold is functioning. We have people in the real businesses, you can learn how to be a businessman and share in the church which is on Sunday and during the week.

I hope I am sharing some revelation; I want to keep it coming from different angles, because until the Spirit of God breaks through into seeing the problem, you won't want to change. I have done itinerate evangelism, I have spoken in the bible schools and I have been to prophetic ministries, I have been to mercy ministries and almost every single ministry under the sun in the body of Christ. To find it in one place? I haven't found it yet. I said Lord you must help us to come together.

## PASTOR'S FRATERNITY

I have seen the pastor and the fraternity sit together and pray in one place. Then you end up in a one man band and you have 2 on staff, then the only way I can get 3 on staff is if my church grows to 300, so they are desperately trying whatever they can to build their numbers, so that they can employ more people. Then when they become too big they don't need to come to the pastor fraternity anymore because they have got their own leadership team. So basically those that come to the fraternity, have got one or two people on staff, they may spend a few months trying to get one meeting but they end up, saying who is going to do the worship? Who is going to do the offering? Who is going to do the preaching? Whose really is going to pray? Who is the head of us? And after spending six month praying and talking about that, you might put together one meeting with 3 of the fraternity. So half the time, these guys are quite lonely because they don't have anyone ministering into their lives, so the organization becomes a place they go to pray for one another.

## The One Man Band

If you are running the church by yourself and you're called the senior pastor, guess what you have to do, you are the paid professional.

you will have people yelling at you saying "we need evangelism", "why are we not discipling people?", "why are we not doing the prophetic?". The poor guy has to preach twice on Sunday, he is holding an elders meeting, a trustees meeting, he is going to do a new believers meeting, if he has got the time to do it. He is also married and with children, and if he has to do the church stuff because everyone works through the day, he will be out every night of the week. He could kiss his wife and kids goodbye because if he is going to see his church grow, he is going to have to be out when people have finished work. This poor soul is going to be working every single night, out training and praying, for Deacons to the point that this poor guy will eventually burn himself out.

So someone comes up with another idea, pastor we should be doing this course, he looks around and everyone has got the idea, they say "there is no training". I want to go to training, please sign my letter, pastor I need to go for this school of training, when they go out, you will never see them again, they end up in their own ministry.

Then the next time them they see them they have to hire them to speak, the pastor himself is barely getting paid, because most of the money is going out of his tithes and offerings into everyone else's ministry doing the work of God. But I'm just left here to shepherd them, so we have pastors burning out having to preach, can't afford to bring in, the Itinerates unless he joins a movement or a mega church.

He then hands up literally running it himself and the poor guy not wanting to hear suggestions from another member of the congregation, please can we do this Father heart stuff? No, can we do this school of supernatural ministry? No, can we do this school of biblical studies? The poor guy is going into shock.

I know what's like, because I have pastored these churches, this guy is literally shaking because the church is never to be run by one man, by a pastor, it was never designed by God, it was never ever in the heart of God. It is to be run by apostles, pastors, prophets, teachers, and evangelists, mercy ministries, administrators, helpers, people of compassion, all of them working together to represent who Christ is. All of them in love, preferring one another, each one of them honoring each other, helping the body become a family, a house of love and healing, a place of deliverance, a place of salvation and a place of holiness.

People say I am the full gospel, I say excuse me, you can't say you have the full gospel if you don't have salvation, pastoral care, teaching, deliverance, apostolic and prophetic, if you don't have all that, you are not the full gospel. A full gospel is the whole package, and you can't be it because you are one person in the full gospel.

I often hear this, I have poured my heart out, I have labored throughout all the camps, each one of them have moved through into uniformity, each one of them trying to throw stones at the other. I am simply hearing the criticizing and judgment from the different groups, they are not doing this, they are not doing that, they see the problem but they don't see the solutions, so they actually become part of the problem by separating themselves from the body. I am not doing that but you are!

# HOUSE CHURCH VS CHURCH MOVEMENT

Do you want to bring wholeness, you must see the revelation of the church with the fivefold and Roman 12. If we get someone saved, what do we do to make sure the person who does gets intricately into relationship in a family? As a friend, work with the pastors, we not talking of one pastor, we can talk of a 100 pastors. For you to have a lot of people being saved, you need a lot people to literally care for them, that is why a home group or a cell group are powerful, and that is why most are meeting in homes.

Then we get the house church movements versus the church movement and that is another complete mess. They met in houses but they also met in the temple, you don't go to one or the other, it's both, the reason why we have the house church movement is because they are frustrated with one man or pastor running the church. It is a reaction, it's not the solution, if we have lots of pastors, we are going to have heaps of home groups, you are going to have all your meetings in the house, training, and caring for them. But the part of the celebration that took place on Sunday, the Sunday service is a place of rejoicing and exalting God, the true discipleship levels down to the home. They met in homes setup under the apostle's teachings, if you don't understand that for the house to be a place of teaching and relationship, then you must understand that those house churches were run under the apostles.

Then if you are not part of the apostles, then you don't actually have any clue of what you are doing because all of this stuff is the problem, house churches are not the solution, big churches are not the solution, the church has to understand that you can have the fivefold in one place.

If you get that revelation by your spirit, you know that you cannot do it by yourself, you need your brother, that is going to take an element of humility, I don't have the full revelation of Christ, I don't know it all, that is a big humble statement. You mean you don't know it all? That means someone else, if I am an evangelist; I need to be working with pastors, I have to be working with prophets and teachers because I cannot bring them to maturity by myself, if I could, I am the full representation of Christ. I have all the ministry, all the gifting and all the calling, that is why Christ was smart enough to make sure that one person didn't get it and call him a Bishop or an Apostle, if he did, then you won't need anyone else.

You will just appoint everyone else to do the job for you because you know it all. The truth is that the apostles have the greatest revelation of how the body works but if he runs it by himself and says I am first, we have another Pyramid structure. The fivefold does not put the apostles on top, the fivefold puts the apostles with the rest of them and Christ as the head of the church.

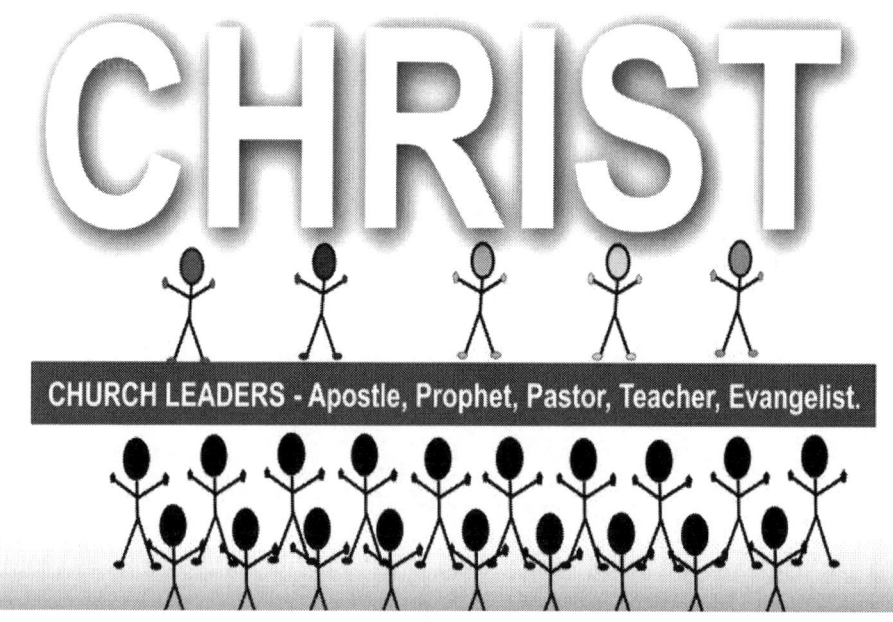

I am hearing teachers say first the apostles, then the prophets, and that pastors, teachers and evangelist are earthly minded. That only apostles and prophets are heavenly minded, they get the blue-print, the revelation and then tell the pastors and teachers how to do it. We have this regional apostle say you can all have your small churches come under me as your apostolic leader and I will now help put your churches in order.

You know what that is? Another form of lordship leadership and it's got nothing to do with the revelation of the fivefold. If you think Christ himself is not heavenly minded, then you don't understand the fivefold. Christ is the pastor, Christ is the evangelist and the teacher, so if you relegate him to the earthly, you miss the fact that Christ himself seated in heaven is the pastor, is the evangelist, and is the teacher.

So you cannot come against the word of God and say only the apostles and prophets are heavenly minded, this is actually a slap in the face and completely contrary to the teaching of Christ. I have seen evangelists that are so heavenly minded, that love souls, they weep, they sow in tears, I have been around pastors who know more about the father heart of God, how to grow up, and about inner healing and of healing the broken heart, they are on the right page, they are heavenly minded. I know teachers, who get revelation of the word of God, you weep when they bring out that breaking of the living bread, the word of God. All of them have to be heavenly minded, all of them have to be seated in heaven by revelation, not the apostles the new kid on the block.

Ten years ago, everyone wanted to be prophets, everything was prophetic, now everything is apostolic; everyone wants to be an apostle. Thank God some are apostles, some are prophets, but Mathew 24 warns us that on the last day, we will have false apostles, false prophets, and false teachers coming to deceive the elect. So make sure you are not tossed every which way, we don't get super apostles, we have apostles, plural not singular.

The Jerusalem church has 12 apostles, the Antioch church has more than one apostle, Paul and Barnabas at-least were two, we know there are apostles in that church because they grew to I think 130,000 people.

# THE DNA OF THE CHURCH

So I am here, I have no problem with a large church, I have no problem with a small church but the problem is, what is the DNA? The DNA is to represent who Christ is, if you don't have the DNA of the fivefold, what you end up having is the problem.

If you are all eyes, then you are prophets, you are not a body. If you are all feet as evangelists, you are not a body. The bible tells us if you think you are part of the body of Christ, you are separate from it if you are all feet, if you are all eyes.

That means the school of prophet is in the Old Testament, not in the New Testament, the New Testament has prophets on staff. I have no problem with training or equipping because we have all activities and disciples but we are not to disciple them to be prophets, you understand that? That is part of it but it is not the fullness, we are to reproduce after our own kind, if you are not in relationship with the others, you will not reproduce a team or the revelation of Christ, you will only reproduce the office of the evangelist. And if you are not in connection with the bride, the body, the building, you will then only reproduce any good people after your own office and you will not be able to equip them into the fullness and maturity of Christ, you will only reproduce after your own kind.

So DNA cannot just be prophetic, cannot just be pastoral, cannot just be teaching, the revelation has to be the DNA of who Christ is, the fullness of the body, He is the head of it, everything comes from Him, the church does not exist apart from Him.

The danger is when we get to programs; we begin to follow signs and wonders. Do you realize that Jesus never built the church on signs and wonders, he moved away from it. If we were in the gospels, we would have built churches around the Mount of Transfiguration and called it the **Glory, Open Heaven Church**. Or we would have called a church after the legions of the demons coming out and we call it the **Deliverance church**. Or we would have built ourselves a church beside the Pool of Siloam, where healings took place; we would have built a healing ministry and called it **Take your Mat and Walk Ministry.** Or if we were there when the fish and loaves were multiplied, we would be called the **Fish and Loaves church**.

Jesus walked away from all the signs and the miracles not because he didn't have the heart for the people, but because he knew that the leadership was not ready to take care of them. He sent them back, he said go back to the priest, go back to the temple, he knew that this team was not yet ready. They were too independent, they were fighting and competing with each other to be the number one. I want to sit at your right hand, I want to sit at your left hand, then mothers are getting involved, I want my son to be in this position. How comes He went up on the mountain? How comes I wasn't there? Jesus had to work with a team, a new wineskin of men to show them the new wine, work within it but he hadn't yet formed the wineskin.

What we tend to do is we want the new wine, that has come into the church for years and I have been in three major moves of God and what ends up happening is the new wine hits the old wines skin, tears it up into pieces, then people say; I don't want the new wine. They blame the move of the Spirit, instead of looking at the fact that leadership structure can't hold the anointing.

Christ is desperately warning us to realize that we do not camp around signs and wonders, we do not camp around your ministry, and we do not camp around miracles. Jesus did greater miracles than most people, the miracle didn't mean they were going to follow him, he healed how many lepers? How many came back, one. Of the 120 people in the upper room which were leaders, he had appointed 84 of them, in literally 3 years of ministry. Only 36 people were added to his ministry, 36 people, he had fed 5,000, he had legions and everybody he prayed for was healed. Do they follow him? No, healings and miracles didn't cause people to follow Christ, you know what did, Love.

Peter eventually got it, you have the words of eternal life, the disciples said we have seen Satan fall from heaven and demons coming out, Jesus said don't rejoice in that, rejoice in the fact that your name is written in heaven in the lamb's book of life, Christ in us, salvation and eternal life. We have to learn how to work together, and not focus upon the power or the ministry.

God help us to get the new wine skin, help us to be humble enough to see that we need each other and the key is how we do that. You must then realize that you are not the fullness and the answer to the church, you are part of the puzzle. So father I pray that you will touch hearts, I pray that you will teach men that are in ministry, those running their own ministry, people who have done global ministry will somehow grip hold of the revelation of this truth and begin to prepare themselves to come together as one, one body, one bride, in Jesus Name.

Amen

Made in the USA
Columbia, SC
22 March 2021